Success Is A Process, Not An Event!

Inspiring A Mindset To Flourish As An Educator

3rd Edition

Mills Carnell Rodgers II

Success Is A Process, Not An Event!

ISBN-13: 9781090705983

DEDICATION

I dedicate this book to my family for the insights and inspiration to pursue this project. I love you!

Success Is A Process, Not An Event!

TABLE OF CONTENTS

Success Is A Process, Not An Event!

INTRODUCTION

Ahh, the good old days in the field of education. Years back, when I was coming up, educators were simply expected to provide instruction and evaluate how well students retained information. Instruction and evaluation tended to be very uniform with little deviation. A typical day of instruction in a middle or high school class consisted of opening a textbook, looking up vocabulary words and/or reading a chapter, a short discussion, and answering the questions at the end of the chapter. Minimal consideration was taken into account in regards to student abilities, learning styles, and other concerns. Each week would wrap up with a test on Friday. I did have a few teachers that were ahead of their time and creative in their approach to teaching, but for the most part, many followed the aforementioned approach.

Fast forward to the present. In addition to instruction, which is now heavily influenced by standardized testing, educators are expected to be de facto counselors, social workers, creative trainers, and more. Teachers are expected to cater to a variety of learning styles and be inclusive of all ability levels. Educators today wear many hats in comparison to their predecessors. Most educators willingly step up to all of these duties out of a passion for helping children. However, it does take a certain mindset and approach to avoid mentally "burning out." *Success Is A Process,*

1

Not An Event, Inspiring A Mindset To Flourish As An Educator, is written by an ACTUAL EDUCATOR who has served in teaching and leadership positions in schools and achievement gap programs. Someone who has actually been on the front lines of education. The purpose of this book is to provide insights and inspiration for educators in order to keep the fire burning and, ultimately, have a positive impact on the students we lead!

Chapter 1

THE WHY

Many couples, when they are expecting a new arrival to the family, have their preference of a boy or girl. We've all heard the many reasons why. For me, that never was a big deal. Heck, it's not like one has any control over it anyway. As a father in waiting, my main concern was to have a healthy child. On November 26, 1997, the night before Thanksgiving, my wishes seemed to come true. The bun, in the form of a 7 pound baby girl, was taken out of the oven (so to speak). Everything was great, 10 fingers, 10 toes, and keeping us up all night like babies are supposed to do

For the first 18 months, everything seemed to be going well. My daughter met all of her milestones on time. She took her first steps near her first birthday. Her interests were typical of any toddler. She loved the go-to toddler favorites of that era, i.e. the Teletubbies and Barney. She had started to say a few words.

Overall, she seemed to be doing well.

We started to notice changes in my daughter around 20 months or so. She had started struggling to sleep at night; she would stay up for a long time. Her speech was not progressing. We took her to the doctor; he said for us to keep a close eye on things and to be observant. Unfortunately, things did not get better. It seemed like she was regressing in many ways.

At this time, I was serving in the Army as a mental health specialist. I was stationed at Fort Leonard Wood, MO, at the Army hospital, working on the psychiatric ward. The internet was really starting to become popular at that time, but I didn't have a computer at home. We had all survived the doom and gloom predictions of Y2K!

It was usually pretty quiet working overnight on the psych ward. Most of us didn't have home computers at that time, so it was a great opportunity for everyone to take turns using the computers on the ward for school work, research, web-surfing, etc. One night at work, I was online; for whatever reason, autism popped into my mind. I had kind of heard a little bit about autism, but was very unfamiliar with it. I just knew that it was something that impacted kids. I decided to look it up. When I started looking at the symptoms, I said to myself, "Oh my god, this seems to be what she has." I scrolled down to see how it was treated, if it was curable. Unfortunately, it wasn't. The pediatrician referred my daughter to the University of Missouri for further testing, where she was officially diagnosed with autism. You talk about a gut punch. Finding out that your child has a disability of that nature definitely changes the trajectory of being a parent.

The reason I share this testimony with you is two-fold. First, it has obviously impacted my family. When you have a child with a disability, life changes but it doesn't change. Let me explain. For example, many considerations are involved in attending a simple outing or get-together that one would not even consider under normal circumstances. You also have all the extra appointments, meetings, etc., that having a family member with a disability involves. And for me, here's the most important detail: LIFE DOES NOT STOP!!!! I know that should go without saying, but I say it anyway because I have encountered people who, while being well meaning, minimize some of the challenges involved. Just like everyone else, raising a child with a disability doesn't mean you are exempt from issues on the job, money troubles, health concerns, car problems, home maintenance, etc. Yes, it seems like common sense, but I bring it up because I have had fellow educators, even those in special education, that unfortunately trivialized and were not empathetic to the challenges the families they serve go through. Plus, you're always concerned about your child's future care. Think about it, most children outlive their parents. Yes, there is a lot to consider.

The second reason has to do with your purpose as an educator. People become educators for a variety of reasons; some are really noble, some are kind of flimsy. This can be said for any occupation. Regardless of one's reason for becoming an educator,

I want to share something with you. My family, like many, depend on educators who are sincere in their desire to nurture the development of the kids they serve. I am so thankful for those educators over the years who texted that my daughter, who has difficulty communicating, did not have money in her lunch account. I appreciate the cafeteria workers who fed her. I respect the bus drivers who got her to school and back safely. I am grateful to the teachers who demonstrated patience while teaching her how to read and write. Look here, I realize not everyone gets into the field of education to do it for 30 years and retire. That is ok. The one thing I do want you to know is that, no matter your reason, you have the ability to truly make a difference in the lives of children and their families in ways that you probably wouldn't think of!!

KEY #1: As educators, we have incredible opportunities to impact lives. How many occupations have significant extended daily interactions with over 100 people for the majority of a year? The only downside is our impact tends to not be realized until years later, when we run into our former students in our communities and they start to share their favorite memories. No doubt though, every teacher has the potential to play a significant role in the lives of the students that enter their classrooms.

ACTION PLAN: What is your purpose for being an educator? What is it that you enjoy the most about being an educator? What do you enjoy the least? Do you see yourself in education in the next 5 years? The next 10 years? These questions should cause you to reflect and give you an idea of the direction you are headed in as an educator and begin to understand where your passion lies.

Mills Carnell Rodgers II

Chapter 2

IT STARTS WITH YOU!

Do you desire to better yourself and your classroom? It all starts with **YOU**. **YOU** must believe in yourself as an educator. **YOU** have to believe what you are doing is going to work. **YOU** have to believe, through your efforts, opportunities will arise that are **FOR YOU**. You have to believe that you are setting your students up for success! Trying to better yourself or situation is never easy. It always requires leaving our comfort zone. It involves the risk of failure. I once heard someone say to be exceptional, you must be the exception. The same can be applied to improving our classrooms and bettering ourselves as educators.

As educators, it is very easy to fall into the mindset of feeling helpless and hopeless. Let's be honest and real. People, who are not educators, are constantly bashing the flaws of our educational system.

"The kids are bad."

"The teachers don't care."

"The teachers are dumb."

"The schools are run down."

Unfortunately, these are some of the common refrains thrown around by the general public and even our leaders. There is a slight degree of truth in each of these statements, dependent on campus and location. You can have a bad teacher or two at any campus. You will have difficult students at the best of schools. Not every campus will be a state of the art facility. There always seems to be a lot of negativity in the general perceptions of education.

Well, despite these perceptions, the reality is an education in the United States is the one reliable institution that provides a viable foundation for the have-nots to join those that have. That is something that ALL educators should be proud of.

It is easy to say we want to be better educators, but it is a challenge to actually make it a reality. Every school year starts off with lofty personal and organizational goals; unfortunately, many of us fall short on a personal and/or organizational level by the end of the school year. I'm of the opinion that our focus needs to be more on the process or progress towards our goals as opposed to the actual goals themselves. Notice that I say progress. Progress indicates positive, consistent actions toward an expectation or goal. We have a much greater likelihood of sticking with our goals, no matter what they are, if we are focused more on the consistent actions to reach a goal. Consistency in our actions leads to growing confidence, which strengthens our resolve in progressing toward our goals.

What follows are strategies that can help us to focus on what is within our power to control:

1. **Believe In YOU.** First and foremost, you have to believe that what you are doing is going to result in success in some form or fashion. You can't rely on others to always spur you into action. It is great to have a support system, but it is meaningless if you don't believe in yourself. Others can encourage, but you have to act. Everything starts and ends with you!

2. **Tune out the Noise.** Just like there is negativity by the general public toward education, there will be some negativity on campus. We've all heard the advice to stay out of the teachers' lounge. I'm not going to be one of those people that says to not visit the teacher's lounge to avoid the "Debbie Downers; I actually got a lot of support and advice in the teachers' lounge as a young teacher. However, there will be those teachers that will make you say to yourself, "Why don't they just retire or quit?" Steer clear of the "Debbie

Downers" wherever they may be found. We tend to become what we constantly hear and see. If you hear enough negativity, you will likely become negative. Like they saying goes, "If you hang around the barbershop, you'll eventually get a haircut."

3. **Keep an Open Mind.** Do your research. Continue to learn about being an educator. Yes, educators are bombarded with professional development. It can be overwhelming at times. You may feel that it is too complicated to implement in your classroom. You may also feel it doesn't fit with your approach as an educator (see #5). It's absolutely normal to feel this way; however, don't discount anything that will help you to better educate students. Also, take the initiative to improve yourself at your craft. There are so many resources online. Through your own research and observation, you may find your own way of doing it that works well for your situation.

4. **Have a positive attitude.** You must believe in what you are doing. You must have a can-do attitude. The glass is half full, not half empty. Being positive doesn't mean you are unaware of challenges or that bad things won't happen to you. You will have setbacks. Exceptional people don't dwell on their setbacks or do

much complaining.

5. **Understand your strengths.** Be yourself as an educator. What is it that you do well? What makes you able to relate to kids? There are certain characteristics that ALL quality educators should have (good classroom management, content knowledge), but that doesn't mean we aren't individuals. When I look at the busy street nearby in my city, I see 5 fast food restaurants that sell burgers within approximately 1 mile of each other. And they are all profitable. They all sell burgers, but put their own unique spin on how the burgers are presented to customers. There is always room for your own unique approach in the classroom, what you bring to the table. Sometimes it takes a while to discover how to fit who you are into providing a classroom that maximizes effective learning.

6. **Work hard.** You will put in the work if you are passionate about what you do. In education, passion can reveal itself through different avenues. Some teachers are passionate about the content they teach. Others are passionate about teaching others. There are some who are passionate about connecting with students. There is no way around it; you have to put forth a high degree of consistent effort at whatever you

do in order to be successful. Even with that, you will still have your ups and downs.

7. **Faith.**   Hey, let's face it; being an educator will test you emotionally and spiritually. It will likely take a belief in something outside of yourself, while believing you are serving a higher purpose, in order to keep yourself going as an educator.

Empower yourself by focusing on what you have control over so that you can positively impact the kids in your classroom!

KEY #2: Understanding the power you have, your beliefs, and who you are, is the catalyst to navigate your road to success, ultimately impacting the kids you serve. As educators, there are numerous circumstances and policies that can have an influence on our actions but, ultimately, we all have to make choices on how we will respond to situations and how we will take action. NO ONE else can do this for you!

ACTION PLAN: Taking action is key to becoming empowered. What are two positive habits you can acquire, in the short term, to increase your self-confidence so that you can take more responsibility and become empowered as an educator?

Success Is A Process, Not An Event!

Chapter 3

THE START OF A NEW SEASON

The beginning of September signals the start of one of our country's favorite past times ....football season! Over the years, I have seen how sports can provide such great analogies for life in general. Just like the start of a sports season, our lives can be broken down into seasons: a new year, the start of a new job, a new relationship........ the start of a new school year! The examples are endless.

There are many lessons that can be learned in equating the start of the football season to the various seasons and cycles in our lives. What follows is a list of situations that a football team encounters during a typical season that equates to what we experience in a school year:

1. **Importance of preparation.** Every team has prepared by learning and training during the offseason. Each team has spent many hours doing conditioning and learning plays. A lack of preparation will definitely insure that the team will be unsuccessful. Same with us on an individual and professional level. We cannot take advantage of an opportunity if we are unprepared mentally, physically, emotionally, etc. We must commit ourselves to learning and improvement. As educators, our summers are spent recharging physically and mentally. We may work during the summers, but it is usually not to the same intensity level as the regular school year. We also may attend trainings during this time to better ourselves as educators. Then there's the always fun week or two before students return to school in which we receive more training and information. This is all done in preparation for the school year to improve our skills in educating children. Proper preparation leads to self-discipline and accountability.

2. **Losing (disappointment).** During a sports season, most teams will lose at least once. It is rare that a team makes it through a season undefeated. A few years ago, the New York Giants won the Super Bowl having lost half of their regular season games. In life, and as educators, we will suffer disappointments. There will

be those days where the lessons do not go as planned. We will have to deal with frustrating student behaviors. Paperwork will be overwhelming. You will wonder what in the heck made me sign up for this. Well, I have good news for you! Like the New York Giants, we do not need to be close to perfect to succeed as educators. We must display consistent competency as opposed to perfection (except when being observed LOL). There will be rough days, but it is important to understand that it is a part of the process. More importantly, we must develop the mental stamina to deal with the disappointments which may arise.

3. **Injuries (unexpected challenges).** Teams will have key players that get injured. It's a kind of paradox. No one hopes for this to happen, but it is expected. Those teams that have good systems in place always seem to suffer less of an impact when this happens. This definitely relates to preparation and foresight. Disclaimer: There are things that happen to us, just like an injury to a key player on a team, which can derail a whole season: health issues, natural disasters, etc. Let's be honest, we are resilient; we are able to recover from many things that happen to us, but it can be extremely challenging in terms of effort, time, and our emotions. We want to focus on things within our circle of control.

This is where preparation helps (See number 1).

4. **One Game at a Time (the process).** A team must focus on winning the game at hand, not the game that is 3 weeks from now or the championship. Winning the game at hand puts the team closer to the goal of making the playoffs or winning a title. This concept applies to us as educators on an individual level. We must focus on the steps to accomplishing our goal as opposed to the actual goal itself. The elephant in the room for educators tends to be standardized test scores. Well, I guess standardized tests aren't really the elephant in the room since they are constantly talked about. While standardized test scores have a significant influence on the reputation of educators and campuses, the reality is that educators have to be effective daily. We still need to be prepared and have the proper energy for the kids we educate. We must focus on the day to day operations of our classrooms. There is nothing wrong with setting goals at the beginning of the school year, but the emphasis has to be on being competent daily. Mastering certain skills and strategies are the keys to accomplishment. A great example for this concept is weight loss. A common New Year's resolution is to lose ___ lbs. by summertime. There is absolutely nothing wrong with setting this goal. However, the

focus has to be more on "how" you will reach that goal and "what" you will do. What is your plan for dieting? Is it reasonable? What is your exercise plan? The consistency in implementation will help you reach your goal more than simply creating a goal. This same principle applies to teaching in the classroom.

While we're talking about consistency in our season, let's touch on the concept of effort. How many times have you heard someone say the following?

"Do your best!"

"Give 100%!"

"You must give it your all, all of the time!"

I'm sure you have heard those clichés numerous times; we should be following them, right? While they are meant to be encouraging, they can also be discouraging. You might be thinking to yourself, "How is that?" Well, here is the reality. We have all watched sporting events in which a team or athlete may simply have a bad day, despite their best efforts, for reasons that are often unknown to the general public. The same can apply to us in our lives. Your "100%" can vary from day to day, based on a number of factors. You may have a "good night's rest, I'm in love, pay day, absolutely best day 100%." Or you may have a "sick/injured, slept 2 hours last night, car won't start, bad day

100%." If you think that you have to be at your "best day 100%" every day, you are likely setting yourself up for disappointment. Your best day does not occur every day, so for you to perform at the "100%" of your best day, every day, is unrealistic and self-defeating. However, you can realistically perform at 100% everyday based on how you are feeling or what you are going through for THAT PARTICULAR DAY! You can be the best you can be for that particular situation. It may not be your all-time best, but it is your best for that moment! We all have to deal with adversity in our lives, just like a team has to deal with adversity during a season. Yet, we can all come out of it as champions!

KEY #3: Whatever goal, dream, or objective you pursue, you will experience highs and lows. The lessons we learn from our disappointments can lead to growth. While your 100% best can vary from day to day based on a number of factors, you can still give your best every day. The key is to stay reasonably consistent in our habits to accomplish our goals.

ACTION PLAN: Throughout the school year, there will inevitably be challenges. While we might not know the exact circumstances of challenges, we can have an idea of what they may be. What are some things that may occur throughout the

school year? What are some strategies that you can use to push through?

Mills Carnell Rodgers II

Chapter 4

GOOD THINGS ARE SUPPOSED TO HAPPEN TO ME!

Les Brown is my absolute favorite motivational speaker. I see him as the Michael Jordan of speakers. His versatility and ability to relate to a variety of audiences is unmatched, in my opinion. He is the G.O.A.T. (Greatest Of All Time). Anyhow, enough of my motivational speaking man crush on Les Brown.

One day, I was watching a motivational video of Les Brown on YouTube. YouTube is such an awesome resource; I wish it was around back in the day when I was coming up. Anyway, in the video, Mr. Brown instructed the audience to say "Good things are supposed to happen to me." He recommended that the audience say this to themselves daily.

Brown went on to say we tend to anticipate bad things happening to us, so we need to affirm the positive. It got me to thinking: do we really expect bad things to happen to us? Or do we expect that good things will NOT happen for us? I don't think we expect tragedy to occur in our lives, but we don't expect to have things go our way. We don't expect to get "lucky." There is a perverted comfort in this approach to our mindset. If you condition yourself not to expect a lot out of life, I guess you can avoid disappointment. Disappointment is a difficult pill to swallow. No one enjoys disappointment. After suffering repeated disappointments, we tend to want to avoid it at all costs. That is why so many people turn to substances to avoid dealing with the pain of past and present disappointments.

So we may not expect tragic things to happen, but we don't expect good things to happen as a way of guarding against disappointment. The unfortunate thing about this type of mental conditioning is that it undermines ambition and hope. I'm sure most of you have heard that if you don't expect to succeed at something, you likely won't. If you don't have the expectation, it is unlikely you will put forth the required effort and persistence that is needed. You've never heard an athlete, after winning a game, title, etc., say that they didn't expect or deserve to win. They almost always say they believed in themselves, even if no one else did. It all starts with a belief.

In his speech, Les Brown was emphasizing the importance of being positive, making affirmations. Affirmations are designed to change our subconscious thoughts by constantly referring to them in our conscious minds. Our subconscious impacts us in ways we are unaware of. We tend to have thought patterns and experiences in our past which, if we are not aware, can undermine our conscious efforts to do better in the present. By constantly affirming the positive, the goal is to change our inner dialogue. What we hear repeatedly tends to impact us.

A positive example I have of this is in my classroom. Sometimes I will play motivational speeches in the background as students work independently. One of the students shared with me that she was studying one night and was falling asleep; however, she recalled one of the speeches I played in class that said you have to push through when you feel like giving up. It prompted her to resume studying! Hearing her say that was like music to my ears; it definitely encouraged me to keep playing those speeches.

So what happens when we start to internalize the message that "good things are supposed to happen to me?" Does that mean everything we pursue will happen? Of course doesn't! Does it mean that you won't be disappointed? Absolutely not! There are some people who suffer through some truly horrific circumstances in their lives, but are seemingly happy. Then, there are some who had a lot of things in their favor and are unhappy. Heck, I remember watching a program where the person acknowledged they had a great upbringing: loving & understanding parents, money, good schools, health, etc. However, can you believe they actually said that having that upbringing, one which seems to elude many of us, was a problem? Really??? Perfect example of how perception shapes our reality. If you choose to see something as a problem, it is a problem. To change our lives, it helps to change our perceptions.

What about those times where will are treated unfairly because of reasons outside of our control, for simply being who we are? I will be honest. Many of us, including myself, have experienced being treated unfairly because of gender, race, country of origin, and sexuality, among many other reasons. This treatment is typically grounded in stereotypes and cultural conditioning. Trust me, I understand how it is unfair and can make one a skeptic. Thankfully, we have many of people who have achieved great things, despite the evils of discrimination. There are well known examples, but there are many more that can be found in our local communities and our own families.

You have to believe in a force outside of yourself to have a high level of positivity. There needs to be a spiritual, but not necessarily religious, component to this. People who believe good things will happen for them will start to become more perceptive of opportunities. They will also tend to attract those people who genuinely can help them.

There is a flip side to this type of thinking. If you truly believe good things are supposed to happen for you, then you will believe that if something doesn't happen, it just wasn't a good thing. I'll keep it real with you, sometimes this is a hard pill to swallow if you are in a desperate situation or have tried repeatedly at something. It's OK to feel disappointment, but we can't let it keep us down. In this day and age, we have many opportunities to overcome our circumstances and do well. It can happen when we exude a faithful, positive mindset, with efforts to match!

So you may be thinking to yourself, "This is all fine and dandy, but how does all this stuff apply to my class of 25 kids?" I don't want to jump the gun, but, as educators, we are leaders of our classrooms (see chapter 6). We are the tone setters. We have to consistently represent and convey a can-do attitude to our students. It's a common refrain in teachers' lounges to hear how the students won't listen, they don't care, etc. Now, I will be realistic; there will be a certain percentage of students who will be extremely challenging to reach, no matter what you do. However, I would be willing to bet that the percentage of those students is very small, much lower than you would think. We must be on guard to not let the proverbial rotten apple spoil our opinion of the bunch. The overwhelming majority of kids want to do the right thing. They will take their cue from us. I will discuss this more in Chapter 6.

The bottom line is that we must be positive and believe in our students in order to get positive results. On a more introspective note, we should continually be working on improving ourselves mentally, spiritually, and physically. In addition to the obvious personal benefits, it helps us to be better educators in the classroom since we are extending ourselves in the same way we are asking our students to extend themselves. Positivity is contagious!

KEY #4: You have to believe that it is your destiny to eventually come out on top. Skeptics will say that this is

unrealistic, you're not facing the reality that bad things can happen. Not true!!! The skeptics are unrealistic; they aren't facing the reality that good things can happen! If you fail, you must have the attitude that it needed to happen in order for you to get to where you want to be. You must believe success is a birthright!

ACTION PLAN: Unfortunately, many of us have been conditioned to believe things aren't supposed to go our way. However, as educators, we are expected to be the ray of hope for the students and families we work with. To be effective educators, we must work on being positive, even when it is not easy. Some of us bring baggage that impacts our mindset, which can have negative results with our students. Self-care and teacher wellness is very important. What are some strategies we can use to reprogram our minds for positivity?

Chapter 5

ASSEMBLY REQUIRED- THE TOOLBOX

On Christmas day, I, like many parents, seem to always spend a significant portion of my day reading directions and putting together gifts which require assembly. It seems as though it is becoming more difficult to remove toys from packages and put things together. I swear, I think you need strength training to open up some of these toy packages. Parents of young kids will definitely know what I'm talking about. And let's not talk about assembly. I think all parents will soon need an engineering degree to put a lot of these toys together. OK, enough griping on my part.

My youngest daughter received a desk for a recent Christmas. I braced myself for the worst. I pulled out the instructions. I started to put the desk together. Surprisingly, the instructions were fairly easy to follow; but as anyone who has assembled furniture knows, it can be time consuming. The life of being a parent on Christmas, spending a portion of your day doing hard work!

The last step in assembling the desk was attaching it to a wall. The instructions recommended a specifically sized drill bit to drill holes and attach the desk. Of course, I did not have that size; I had a drill bit that was close to the recommended size. I knew I could not go out and purchase the recommended bit on Christmas Day. Even in this day and age, all the stores are actually closed on Christmas! I attempted a number of alternatives, hoping they would work. I probably spent an hour or so trying different options, to no avail. After trying alternatives, without much more I could do, I decided to try the drill bit I had. It was not the size the instructions recommended, but it was close. Guess what? It worked just fine!

This situation is very symbolic of what happens on a daily basis in our lives and classrooms. Many of us have wants, desires, and goals. We are often looking for ideal solutions to our goals, problems, etc. Many times, the ideal solution is not available. However, we often have what we need within our grasp! Especially in today's day and age, the right people, knowledge, and skills can be a few clicks of a mouse or taps on a smartphone away. Technology has connected our world and opened doors that were not available several years ago. We have incredible access to information nowadays, compared to when I was coming up back in the day. Finding information was so much more challenging back then. Now, the help we need to start our goals is at our fingertips from the comfort of wherever we are located.

I did not have the recommended or ideal tool for attaching the desk to the wall, but what I did have was good enough. We may not have the absolute, best resources for what we are looking to accomplish, but we usually have enough to get started. I have seen so many instances where people are trying to put the "perfect" plan together. Because of this, it takes them forever to get started. Then, when they finally start, they encounter situations that they had not planned for. I guess my point is that it is much better to come up with a solid plan, not a perfect plan, and implement it. You are going to have to make adjustments along the way anyhow. Sports is a great example of this concept. A coach will create a game plan for a team. For example, a football coach may go into a game with strategy of wanting to pass the ball the majority of the game because he knows his opponent has a weak passing defense. However, come the day of the game, the weather may not make passing the ball a viable option. A good coach will make adjustments based on the situation at hand, despite what they planned for. We can apply this same principle to our lives. IT IS IMPORTANT TO SIMPLY START AND/OR TAKE ACTION! Do what you can with what you have.

In education, we are often lacking in resources because of funding situations, which can vary from state to state. Actually, it can vary from district to district in the same city. Funding often relates to the socioeconomic characteristics of the community served. Unfortunately, it can become a situation of the haves and have nots. Even though there are discrepancies in resources, the reality is that kids can still receive a quality education with teachers who have the right attitudes along with competence. We, as educators, have what is needed to prepare our kids. We usually have enough skill and the right attitude to prepare kids for the future. Yes, it would be great if more money was being poured in for resources at schools. I'll go on record by saying we should put more money into education. Regardless, we can still have a positive impact on kids, families, and communities with the resources that are available. YOU HAVE WHAT IT TAKES!! No doubt, this can obviously impact the quality and diversity of education.

My youngest daughter is a level 6 gymnast. She has been in gymnastics since the age of 3. As a result, I've had the opportunity to go to numerous competitions. If you've ever been to or witnessed a gymnastics meet, you were probably amazed at the level of skill the gymnasts display to perform their routines. It is quite incredible. The athletes must remember the moves and perform them competently and safely. Gymnasts practice many hours a week, even at a young age. My daughter practiced 3.5 hours a day, 5 days a week, as a level 5 gymnast, at 8 years old. This is in addition to having a full day of school. I have always admired her commitment for hanging with it.

At the end of every meet, as you likely already know, medals are given for 1st place, 2nd place, and so on. There are usually 10-20 gymnasts competing for medals based on skill level and age at a typical gymnastics meet. The gymnasts receive placement medals for individual events and for overall scores. Because of the volume of participants, it is difficult to keep track of the placements until they are announced at the end.

I was attending a Level 4 meet for my daughter. I thought she had competed well and was anticipating the results. They started to announce the placements of the gymnasts, first place all the way to fifteenth place for the various events and categories. While they were announcing the placements, something occurred to me. In that moment, I realized that most of these young ladies were all very skilled and performed the events without any obvious flaws. They could all do the moves and skills. To the untrained eye, practically every gymnasts would be touted as a future Olympian. However, there was 1st place, 2nd place, 3rd place, and so on. It was something small that separated each one from being that 1st place or 7th place finisher. Something that most of us would not even be able to recognize. We have all heard that you have to put in work to be great; however, the visualization of seeing all of these very competent gymnasts being ranked really made me reflect upon that concept.

Let's relate this to the classroom. As educators, we are expected to attend professional development. At these trainings, we often receive a lot of strategies and resources, especially since technology makes these readily available nowadays; but let's be honest. Sometimes, it can often be a bit much. I know I have sat in trainings, especially as a young educator, and thought, "This is cool, but how can I really use this?" As I became a more experienced educator, I learned that it did not take wholesale changes to improve classroom management and instruction. More than anything, it took consistency.

I've had plenty of opportunities to observe teachers in formal and informal capacities as an instructional coach, substitute administrator, and even as an inclusion teacher. Being an inclusion teacher was probably one of the best things that could happen to me before becoming a general ed teacher; I had the opportunity to see a wide variety of teaching styles and practices. From my observations, the one constant in struggling classrooms was a lack of consistency. Those teachers that were very effective were consistent with expectations and procedures.

Something that I don't hear often, but needs to be mentioned, is the self-discipline of teachers in regards to the actual operation of a classroom. IT ACTUALLY TAKES A CERTAIN DEGREE OF SELF-DISCIPLINE ON THE TEACHER'S PART TO RUN A CLASSROOM. Teachers who struggle usually have an idea of what needs to be improved, but have problems with implementation or simply sticking with it. Let's be honest…. we're all at a variety of stages of personal development. Who we are as a person, in terms of self-development, impacts the type of educator we are because of values. Our shortcomings have the potential to be manifested in how we lead our classrooms. As leaders of our classrooms, we must have a level of awareness and accountability to work on minimizing our personal flaws so that they do not impact the students we educate. That includes biases, stereotypes, and cultural conditioning.

We must use the tools that are available in our toolbox. Yes, we can use the shiniest, brightest resources; however, what we have is usually enough to make a great impact. You have what it takes!!!!

KEY #5: We probably don't have the ideal resources for reaching our aspirations, but we usually have enough to get from point A to point B or even C. The mistake so many people make when they are pursuing a goal is believing that everything should be perfect. WRONG!!! The best thing is to start; there will be so many unforeseen situations that you could have never predicted or thought to prepare for........it's part of the process! That is how you learn and grow.

ACTION PLAN: What are some resources you have available to you that you can use immediately to start on your path to success? Are there people who can offer support in the form of knowledge, and mentorship, without expecting something in return?

Mills Carnell Rodgers II

Chapter 6

FOLLOW THE LEADER

Anyone who has served any amount of time in the military knows that there is always constant change in the personnel of your unit. Coworkers, subordinates, and leaders are always coming and going to new assignments. You have the opportunity to work with so many different people with varying approaches to their work, even though the military is based on uniformity.

I served 5 years in the US Army as a mental health specialist, which is basically a counselor. During this time, I had an opportunity to work with a leader who has impacted me more than any other in terms of his approach to leadership. His name was SFC Eastman. He was assigned to take over (NCOIC for my military folks) the Behavioral Science department at the facility I was assigned. I was in my 20s' at the time and was learning a lot about how to function in the real world, being in a leadership position in the department myself.

I remember when SFC Eastman first took over. He was very deliberate in his actions. At the time, I thought he was too deliberate. He was very calm and reserved. He seemed too passive. He asked questions and took notes, but didn't really jump into the functions of our department. As a twentysomething, it seemed kind of weird to me, to say the least. I thought leaders should come in, take charge, and immediately implement their program.

Boy, was I wrong. After about a month or so, SFC Eastman had a meeting with us. He explained that he was observing how we operated and learning our strengths and weaknesses. He then explained how he planned to address areas we could improve upon. He also brought a level of organization to everything we did. It was more work for us; however, the changes were practical, thus everyone embraced the changes. He treated everyone respectfully and with equal importance. SFC Eastman was very firm in his expectations, but reasonable. His approach ultimately made our section much more productive and readied our soldiers for growth professionally. I learned a lot in my short time under SFC Eastman about leadership. He taught me that leaders should take time to be observant and learn all the facts, not to overreact or act in haste. You want to understand the "why" behind how things are functioning. You also want to take time to explain why there are changes, since it builds buy in and trust. SFC Eastman made a lasting impact on me.

Whether you like it or not, we are all leaders. I actually created an acronym that aligns with that idea; it uses the name of a great Ivy League college: Y.A.L.E. - You Are Leaders Every day. We are leaders of our families. We are leaders of teams on our jobs. We are leaders in our communities. Yes, we are leaders in our classrooms.

Something unfortunate that I have noticed in education is that some teachers do not see themselves as leaders, despite the fact that they are often teaching over 100 students per day at the secondary levels. They often view themselves as cogs in the wheel, part of a system. There is a degree of truth in that belief, but here's the reality. There aren't many occupations out there that allow you to have that sort of direct, consistent impact with that amount of people. Think about it: for 9 months or so, a teacher has the opportunity to have significant interactions with the students in their classrooms that can impact those kids for a lifetime. Most people, after many years, can still name the majority, if not all, of their teachers. To me, that's incredible!

I think it is important for teachers to see themselves as leaders because they ARE leaders. I believe seeing yourself as a leader brings about a heightened sense of awareness about oneself and surroundings. Just imagine if everyone functioned as if they were an exceptional leader. Notice I said exceptional; I'm not talking about having the qualities of the dreaded bad boss. I'm talking about high quality leaders.

What qualities make great leaders? Leaders are faced with

significant challenges, temptations, and responsibilities at any level. Aren't those the same obstacles that we face on a personal level? Essentially, if we can start to embody the qualities of great leadership, we can ultimately improve ourselves, classrooms, and campuses. I hate to use "principalspeak," but there are only a handful of administrators on a campus and dozens of teachers. It is very difficult for administrators to regulate all happenings on a campus. Effective leadership from teachers can positively impact a campus. One message to administrators, though: you have to place trust in your faculty by allowing them to take the chances that effective leaders often do. You cannot micromanage; that will sink morale instantly and will likely not get the results you are seeking.

Here are a few qualities I have observed and appreciate of effective leaders, which we should embody as educators:

1. **Communication.** I'm sure that is a huge surprise, right? Seriously, we all need the ability to effectively communicate our needs and messages. Most people tend to think of communication as simply one's ability to deliver information; of course, this is a big part of being an educator. However, a large part of communication is the ability to receive and interpret information. Unfortunately, for many of us, this is a skill that could use more development. As educators, we must be skilled in interpreting words and behaviors

of our students, who are often at stages in their development in which it is very difficult for them to articulate their thoughts and needs. In being an effective communicator, you also must have the ability to determine the real meaning or purpose of communication. Teachers and leaders must have a "counselor like" ability to find meaning in words and actions of students that, in many cases, students are not even aware of themselves. Communication occurs verbally and non-verbally. Non-verbals are probably more significant than the actual words we speak. If our nonverbals (body language, expression, posture, etc.) don't align with our spoken words, the verbals instantly lose credibility. We all know of people who "beat around the bush" when attempting to make a point. Or they are not direct in their communication because they don't want to be offensive. An effective leader will have an ability to listen and value input, regardless of person or position. Great insights can come from all directions, even our students. Don't be afraid or insecure in implementing an idea that one of your kids thought up. It can really build rapport and trust in the classroom, ultimately improving willingness to listen and learn. Communication is important for personal & professional growth as an educator.

2. **Vision.** A great leader is able to "rally the troops." In life, subordinates, and people in general, get so wrapped up in the day to day grind of living and working that we sometimes lose focus of the big picture. A great leader will put people in a position to maximize their contribution based on their abilities. As individuals, like leaders of an organization, we must identify our purpose regularly while being focused on the process.

3. **Prioritization.** Prioritization is related to vision. To prioritize is to understand what needs attention and what actions will yield the greatest positive impact. Prioritization is one of the most important duties of a leader, in my opinion. Most people tend to believe that whatever they are working on is of utmost importance to their group, team, family, etc. Sometimes, there is truth to that but, in most cases, we tend to overestimate our importance. Don't get me wrong, what we do may be important, but not as much as we think. We all know of people who blow everything out of proportion. Everything is an emergency. Every situation needs immediate attention. The sky is always falling. Great leaders are able to redirect. Through prioritization, a great leader can figure out what deserves immediate attention. Every situation does not require the same

time and energy. We must use prioritization on a personal and professional level also.

4. **Pragmatism.** I think pragmatism is such a neat word. I had not heard of the word (or at least was not paying attention) until I heard a college instructor use it when I was working on my master's degree. Pragmatic is basically another way of saying practicality based on need. A leader must do what is practical, sometimes deviating from the ideal, in doing what is needed. Sometimes you find leaders and people who are so bound to a particular philosophy that they cannot deviate from it, even though staying put may mean obvious consequences. Good examples of pragmatism are found in the sports world. Bill Belichick of the NFL's New England Patriots is an example of a coach who is pragmatic in his approach to game planning. The Patriots have been the top franchise in a sport that is very difficult to perform at a high level over an extended period of time. One of the reasons is that he adjusts to the strengths of the players on his roster (to fit the vision), as opposed to making the players adapt to a particular style of play. Yes, Belichick has had Tom Brady, one of the best quarterbacks to play the game. However, there have been other quarterbacks, who would be considered all-time greats, on teams that

haven't experienced nearly the success that the Patriots have had under Belichick. One thing that most players who have played under Belichick mention is that he finds what they do well and puts them in positon to use their strengths. Because of this ability to understand talents and make adjustments, the Patriots have managed to be considered one of the top franchises in sports. With pragmatism, there are certain things that are non-negotiables, like discipline and accountability. Whether leading your classroom, family, or any group, those qualities cannot and should not be sacrificed. In summary, we all must be insightful enough to make adjustments when necessary.

5. **Perspective.** Perspective kind of ties in with prioritization (see number 3). Great leaders do not overreact or make impulsive decisions. Leaders are the gatekeepers of the vision of an organization. When others may feel concern or start to panic, a great leader is able to take in all information, make a sound decision, and sell that decision to the people they lead. A great leader has the tendency to look at the upside of a situation, even if it is negative. They typically have a can do attitude and emphasize overcoming the obstacles to be victorious in the end. Great teachers must have this quality. Our students come to us with all sorts of

issues. We must take them as they are and work with them. We must see the glass as half full. Your so called realist will say that is not reality, you have to call a spade a spade. Keeping a positive perspective does not mean you are ignoring the realities of a situation. It takes a positive perspective to overcome negative situations. You have to think you can do something in order to do it. If you don't think you can do something, chances are you won't be able to do it because you will lack effort or not even trying because of lack of belief. The same growth mindset that we teach kids needs to apply to us as professionals. Perspective is important on a personal and professional level.

6. **Consistency.** Here I go again talking about consistency, but it is so important in terms of success. The saying goes that slow and steady wins the race....shouldn't the saying be nice and steady? Who really wants slow? Regardless, the idea behind that saying is the importance of being consistent. Many times we tend to put a lot of energy into getting off to a fast start or finishing strong. Not to throw shade, but it kind of tickles me when I hear teachers talk about how great the kids are during the first few weeks of school. Of course they are good. Teachers are usually focused on implementing classroom procedures; students are

feeling teachers out. That combination will usually bring out the best in students. In my observations as an instructional coach and program lead, teachers start to fall short because of inconsistent policy and procedures in the classroom. Some teachers fall victim to how well behaved students are during the first few weeks of school, when procedures are emphasized, and start to not enforce those same policies. Unfortunately, that's when the problems start. Let me share something with you: students respect consistency and predictability, even if they don't express it outwardly.

Again, consistency is such an important concept because it is tied in to action and value. We all value consistency.........the restaurant that regularly provides quality meals, the sports team that is always competitive, the cell phone with reliable reception, just to name a few examples. Who enjoys a team who wins 2 out of 10 games, even if the 2 victories are huge? Who wants to go to restaurant that gets the order right 1 out of 5 visits? Consistency doesn't mean perfection, because everything and everyone is capable of coming up short from time to time; but we should deliver to ourselves and others regularly. Great leaders and great people are incredibly consistent to the point of being predictable. You have to be capable of delivering to yourself and to others.

Quick story about consistency and structure. I was asked by my principal to take on leading our campus's credit recovery program, which is called Achieve. Many teachers frown on that position since you have to deal with a lot of students who struggle for a variety of reasons. Many of the students are in Achieve for attendance and academic issues. Because of poor attendance, these students have struggled academically. There are a significant amount of students who have honestly made bad choices by not attending classes as required. Of course, if you aren't attending class, it is pretty difficult to learn the material. Achieve is kind of the "last chance" for students that are short of credits. Many of these students are in danger of ultimately dropping out if they are unable to recover the credits. Achieve is basically a dropout prevention program. Achieve will be referenced on occasion throughout this book.

After taking over the program, one of the things I observed was a need for structure and motivation. The kids that are in Achieve struggle with motivation, even though it is their "last chance." As a result, I implemented structures to help them make progress. Naturally, some of the kids were extremely vocal in their displeasure with the changes; however, by the end of the year, those kids were most appreciative.

Students crave predictability and consistency at school. Deep down, they hate chaotic classrooms. I've heard kids complain about how some teachers let students do whatever they want or don't give enough work. You're probably saying to yourself, "Dude, you're lying." I kid you not, students have complained numerous times; no matter their attitudes or behaviors, they expect teachers to professional by providing quality instruction, even if they chose to not do the work. They don't want you to be too cool; they want you to act like an older person LOL. Kids actually have their own expectation in regards to the profile of a teacher. Students want teachers to act like teachers, meaning they want teachers to consistently hold them to expectations, teach, and act like adults. In other words, be a leader!

KEY #6: **A leader is considered anyone who can have an influence or impact on others. Well, guess what? That means you! It seems like it would be a no brainer that teachers are leaders. All of us are leaders. Leaders aren't solely based on authority, in fact, you do not need authority to be a leader. Leadership is about attitude, accountability, and initiative. When we begin to realize how we are potential role models for the people in our lives, we tend to carry ourselves and perform at a higher level.**

ACTION PLAN: **Think of someone you directly impact consistently. It can be a family member, friend, coworker, or your students. Why does that person admire and respect you? How can you continue make a positive impact on this person's life? By making a positive impact, how do you improve your own skills in regards to your aspirations?**

Chapter 7

THE ROAD TO SUCCESS

I once heard a motivational speaker say, "You are going to fail your way to success." Kind of intimidating if you think about it, right? Hearing that might discourage some from even trying to chase their dreams. However, if your mind isn't conditioned to deal with disappointment to some degree, then it probably is not ready for the amount of trial and error needed to become successful. The reality is failure is not enjoyable, under any circumstances. Failure can be a great teacher, but experiencing it just plain sucks! We need to be able to minimize our fear of failure when chasing our goals and dreams.

About a year or so ago, I decided to try my hand at e-commerce. Like any entrepreneur, I wanted to take more control of my destiny. I did my research and figured it was something that

I could do while I maintained employment to bring in some extra income. I decided to sell unused to gently used items from around the house on E-Bay and Amazon. They ended up selling pretty quickly. It seemed like I was on to something. I started to research merchandise I could buy for wholesale at a reasonable price on a limited budget and sell for a profit on the e-commerce sites at a price that was competitive to retailers. Hmm, what could that be? Ties!!! They seemed like the perfect item. You can find decent quality ties at a low price from overseas and easily sale them at a price that was competitive with any retailer here in the United States. Plus, ties are easy to stock and cheap to ship. Brilliant idea, right?

Well, actually it was, but it came with some disclaimers. I did not take into account the amount of competition there is on the e-commerce websites. The internet is a two edged sword. Starting a business is so much more accessible than it was back in the day, which is great because so many more of us have the opportunity to live our dreams; however, the competition has skyrocketed because it is so easy to participate.

After a few months, with disappointing sales, I decided to stop actively pursuing the selling of ties on e-commerce sites. It wasn't worth it for me. I simply didn't have a passion for selling merchandise online, especially with the lack of success I experienced. There was too many things outside of my control in regards to the marketing, algorithms, and all the good stuff that comes into consideration when selling on the internet. I was motivated by the potential income it could provide, but that in and of itself was not enough to drive me to keep actively pursuing that type of business. I can admit I did not succeed at e-commerce. Sometimes, you have to know when to let go. In all honesty, it wasn't something that I was super driven to do. I knew I wanted to do something to create my own income, but decided it wasn't e-commerce of that nature. I learned why people always say to follow your passion. Following your passion will get you through those times when things aren't going quite right, because you truly believe in what you are doing. It will drive you to research, revamp, and resume. After some soul searching, I directed my energies toward something that had a greater relevance for me: coaching, writing, and speaking.

The process of achieving success is filled with numerous challenges. It is easy to have a dream. Making it happen is a different story. Simply wanting is not enough. EVERYONE WANTS! What are you willing to do to get what you want? What are you willing to devote or give up in order to chase your goals or dreams? We must focus more on our process or plan toward our dreams as opposed to the dream itself. We must use the progress we make in our process as motivation. As mentioned earlier, progress indicates positive, consistent actions toward an expectation or goal. We have a much greater likelihood of sticking with our goals if we are focused more on the consistent actions to reach a goal. Consistency in our actions leads to growing confidence, which strengthens our resolve in progressing toward our goals. To be successful, we must consistently make progress. Success doesn't happen overnight; it takes time. There will be trial and error along with disappointments. The road may have detours and delays, but you can reach your destination

Another important concept on the road to success is the myth of perfection. YOU DO NOT HAVE TO BE PERFECT IN ORDER TO BE GREAT OR REACH YOUR GOAL! I think that is important to share because there are many times we quit or don't even try because we feel we're not perfect or have the perfect circumstances. Listen, we all make mistakes. Most of us have experienced deep disappointments, failures, or challenges. Luckily, we have opportunities to succeed in today's world despite this. Sports is a great analogy for understanding that we do not need to be perfect in order to win or be great. Muhammad Ali is considered by many as the greatest boxer of all time; yet, he wasn't undefeated. He wasn't considered a power puncher. Despite this, he is still viewed as the best ever. The Houston Astros won the 2017 MLB World Series. They lost 61 times in the regular season. They experienced failure 61 times in the regular season, yet were able to reach their goal of winning a championship.

I know there are some of you out there who have suffered some losses and abandoned your dreams. I am here to share some good news with you.......you are still on the path to accomplishing your goal! Thank goodness, each day allows an opportunity to resume! Remember, success is a process and not an event. In many cases, the process involves some stumbles, whether it is failure or losing focus. Many people who have achieved great success often had a number of stumbles, challenges, & failures along the way. The success process often requires a lot of trial and error. So celebrate the good news and be rejuvenated & refocused. This is your time to resume your progress on the path to accomplishing your goals. You got what it takes!! Examples abound of imperfect people making an impact and doing great things. Thank God perfection is not needed on the road to success; you only need to stay on the road!

KEY #7: There will be many challenges along the way. You will experience failure. Let's be real......failure does not feel good, even when a valuable lesson is learned. Sometimes we have to try our hands at a number of things in order to figure out what is truly our passion. Keep an open mind. And like I previously mentioned in this book, don't seek perfection prior to getting started with your goals. Life is too short. Continuously seeking perfection will result in a loss of precious time. You will have a learning curve anyway, so you might as well start. The most important thing is to start your journey on the road to success!

ACTION PLAN: Out of the 7 concepts covered by each chapter, which one would you stand to benefit most from? Make that key a point of emphasis in your daily life to help you move toward fulfilling you maximum potential!

Mills Carnell Rodgers II

ABOUT THE AUTHOR

Mills Carnell Rodgers is a speaker and educator in San Antonio, TX, having worked in schools with high at-risk populations throughout his career. He is originally from Ville Platte, LA. As an educator, he has held positions to include special education teacher, general education science teacher, science instructional coach, academic instructional coach, academic coordinator, administrative intern, Achieve coordinator, and substitute assistant principal. "Mr. Rodge" has also served in the US Army as a mental health specialist which, in civilian lingo, is a counselor. He is also a husband and a parent to his 2 daughters. His oldest daughter is diagnosed with moderate to severe autism. Mr. Rodge can honestly say that parenting a child with special needs has so many "behind the scenes" challenges that many people, including educators, overlook. He is compelled to share his insights about being parent to a special needs child with others in order to build awareness and ultimately improve how needs are met for at-risk students in general.

His personal and professional experiences have allowed him to gain some unique insights on a variety of topics that he believes can have a positive impact on the lives of many.

Please contact us if you have any questions, comments, or would like to hire Rodgers Speaks: Mr. Rodge's Neighborhood as a speaker for your organization.

Email: mr-rodge@successisaprocess.net

Phone: (210) 651-2026

Website: www.successisaprocess.net

Facebook/Instagram/Twitter Page: Rodgers Speaks: Mr. Rodge's Neighborhood